America's Security Agencies: The Department of Homeland Security, FBI, NSA, and CIA

The Constitution and the United States Government

THE SECURITY AGENCIES OF THE UNITED STATES: HOW THE CIA, FBI, NSA, AND HOMELAND SECURITY KEEP US SAFE

Tom Streissguth

Enslow Publishers, Inc.
40 Industrial Road
Box 398
Berkeley Heights, NJ 07922
USA

http://www.enslow.com

Original edition published as *America's Security Agencies: The Department of Homeland Security, FBI, NSA, and CIA* in 2008.

Library of Congress Cataloging-in-Publication Data

Streissguth, Thomas, 1958–
 The security agencies of the United States : how the CIA, FBI, NSA and Homeland Security keep us safe / Tom Streissguth.
    p. cm.
 Includes bibliographical references and index.
 Summary: "Read about America's Security Agencies and how they keep us safe"—Provided by publisher.
 ISBN 978-0-7660-4064-9
 1. Intelligence service—United States—Juvenile literature. 2. United States. Central Intelligence Agency—Juvenile literature. 3. United States. Federal Bureau of Investigation—Juvenile literature. 4. United States. National Security Agency—Juvenile literature. 5. United States. Dept. of Homeland Security—Juvenile literature. 6. National security—United States—Juvenile literature. I. Title.
 JK468.I6S76 2012
 355'.033073—dc23
                                          2011028542
Future editions:
Paperback ISBN 978-1-4644-0170-1
ePUB ISBN 978-1-4645-1077-9
PDF ISBN 978-1-4646-1077-6

Printed in the United States of America.

032012 Lake Book Manufacturing, Inc., Melrose Park, IL

10 9 8 7 6 5 4 3 2 1

To Our Readers: We have done our best to make sure all Internet addresses in this book were active and appropriate when we went to press. However, the author and the publisher have no control over and assume no liability for the material available on those Internet sites or on other Web sites they may link to. Any comments or suggestions can be sent by e-mail to comments@enslow.com or to the address on the back cover.

♻ Enslow Publishers, Inc., is committed to printing our books on recycled paper. The paper in every book contains 10% to 30% post-consumer waste (PCW). The cover board on the outside of each book contains 100% PCW. Our goal is to do our part to help young people and the environment too!

Photo Credits: CBP, p. 24; CIA, pp. 38, 41, 49; Department of Defense, p. 34; Courtesy of the Federal Bureau of Investigation, pp. 67, 71, 72, 75, 76, 80, 84–85; Department of Homeland Security, pp. 12–13, 14, 15, 18-19; ©Enslow Publishers, Inc., p. 6; International Security Assistance Force, p. 43; John F. Kennedy Library, p. 27; Library of Congress, pp. 29, 47, 63, 65; National Reconnaissance Office, 42; NSA, pp. 58–59, 60; Shutterstock, pp. 7, 22–23, 78–79.

Cover Photo: ©Peter Kim/Shutterstock

CONTENTS

BRANCHES OF GOVERNMENT

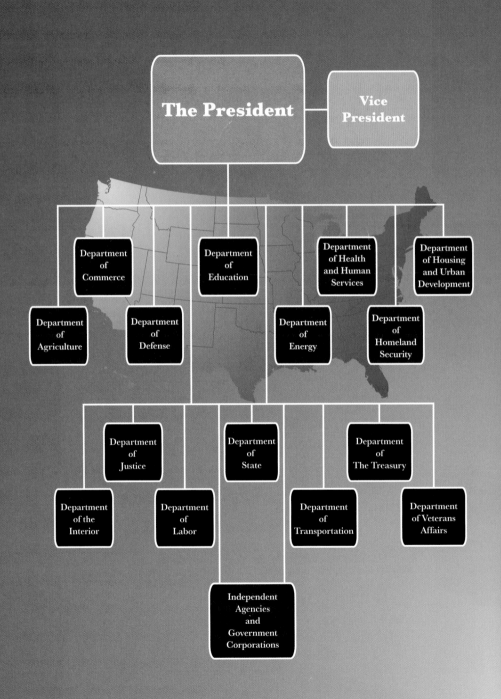

1

The Department of Homeland Security

The morning of September 11, 2001, brought terror from the skies to the eastern United States. Terrorists hijacked four passenger jets. Three of the planes struck buildings in New York City and Arlington, Virginia, just outside of Washington, D.C. Another plane crashed in a field in Pennsylvania before reaching its target.

In New York, fire and police units rushed to the scene. No one was sure what was happening. The city's mayor had no information from the military. Television reporters speculated on the identity of the terrorists.

At the time, President George W. Bush was visiting Sarasota, Florida, far from nation's capital in Washington, D.C.

From Florida, the president flew to an underground bunker in Nebraska. Like the rest of the country, he was struggling to understand the situation. He did not know whether more attacks were coming, and was not sure how the country should respond.[1]

Immediately after the attack, the Federal Aviation Administration (FAA) grounded all planes, except for those used by the military. FAA air-traffic controllers worked with the military to patrol the skies. The military increased security all over the country. Armed guards stood watch at airports, border crossings, and harbors. United States military bases all over the world were put on alert.

The response was slow and uncoordinated. Although some members of the government had received general warnings, the timing and locations of the attack had been a complete surprise. Some information about a plot to hijack planes had arrived from federal agencies such as the Central Intelligence Agency (CIA). But the CIA and the Federal Bureau of Investigation (FBI) learn of such plots all the time. There seemed to not be enough details to warn the agencies about this one. Nobody took much time to investigate it, or to prepare for it.

★ A Color-Coded Warning

On September 20, 2001, nine days after the attacks, President Bush signed an executive order. An executive order is a rule that a president issues that has the force of a law. The order created the Office of Homeland Security (OHS). Bush nominated Tom Ridge, a former governor of Pennsylvania, as the first director of the OHS, which the Senate approved.[2]

The mission of the OHS was to coordinate intelligence and information. The office would try to prevent future terrorist attacks against the United States. It would prepare the states for

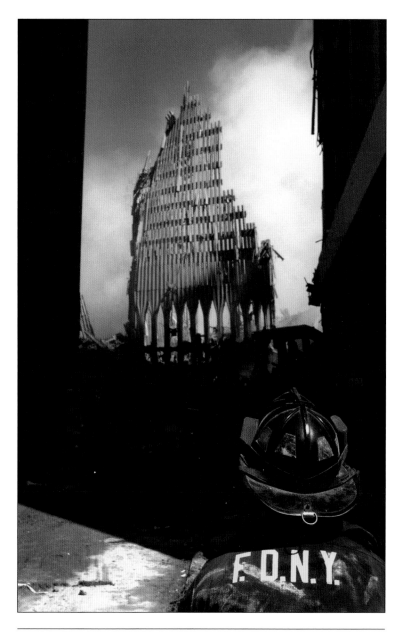

A New York City fire fighter looks up at what remains of the World Trade Center after its collapse during the September 11th terrorist attack. After the 9/11 attacks, then President George W. Bush responded by creating what would become the Department of the Homeland Security.

The National Operations Center (NOC) operates all day, every day. It is an integral part of the Department of Homeland Security, bringing together information from federal, state, local, and private sector agencies to help identify, discourage, and stop terrorist acts and to manage domestic incidents.

a terrorist attack if one was about to occur. After the attack, the office would help local police and fire and rescue departments respond and aid victims.

The agency needed a way to warn people of an expected attack. If it found a terrorist attack in the works, this warning would allow the country to prepare. Fire and police units would go on alert. Everyone would watch for suspicious activity.

In March 2002, the Homeland Security Advisory System started. A presidential directive established this new "risk advisory" scale. Five colors represented five different states of alert:

GREEN Low risk of terrorism

BLUE Guarded (general risk with no credible threats)

YELLOW Significant risk of terrorist attacks

ORANGE High risk of a local terrorist attacks

RED Severe (A terrorist attack has occurred or is about to.)

In November, Congress passed the Homeland Security Act of 2002. This created the Department of Homeland Security (DHS), and made the di-rector of the DHS a member of the president's Cabinet. In January 2003, the Department of Homeland Security began operating the Homeland Security Advisory System. Since the system began, there have been no Red alerts. However, the system flashed Orange when terrorist attacks occurred in foreign countries. Most of the time, as in the summer of 2006, the system showed Yellow, with an "elevated risk" of attacks but none about to occur.[3]

At federal buildings, many security workers took their cue from the warning system. When the warning level reached Orange, for example, they would search all cars that enter the property. The system was, as scheduled, phased out April 27, 2011, and replaced with a new system called the National Terrorism Advisory System. The phase-out was announced on January 27, 2011, by Secretary of Homeland Security Janet Napolitano.

According to Napolitano, the new National Terrorism Advisory System will provide the public and all law enforcement agencies with detailed information about specific or credible terrorist threats. Instead of the old color-coded warnings, the new NTAS alerts will clearly state that there is either an "imminent threat" or "elevated threat." In addition, noted Napolitano, the new NTAS alerts will include a concise summary of the terrorist threat along with the specific steps public safety officials and the public should take in reaction to the threat.

★ A New Department

There was strong debate in the government about what the job of the new agency should be. Some argued that the FBI and the CIA should become part of it. If the work of these large and powerful agencies could be combined, this would help coordinate the preparation for a terrorist attack.

But leaders of the FBI and CIA disagreed. They wanted to keep their work independent. The CIA, in particular, runs many secret operations. It does not want to share its information or methods with any other federal agency.

Congress also debated the rights of the new agency's employees. Federal employees generally enjoy many job protections. They cannot be fired without a good reason. If they are fired, they can appeal the decision. Tom Ridge saw

President George W. Bush signs the Homeland Security Appropriations Act of 2004 at the Department of Homeland Security in Washington, D.C., Wednesday October 1, 2003.

this as an important way of doing things. If his agency lacked such job protection, he believed that it might not attract good workers. Also, citizens who apply to work for the DHS and other security agencies in the federal government go through a rigorous application process. The agency does extensive testing and background checks on each applicant. This decreases the chances that a dishonest or traitorous person would get hired.

★ Some Provisions

Still, President Bush and others believed employees of the new agency should not have such job protection. Employees of a homeland security agency might be incompetent.

Janet Napolitano is the third and current United States Secretary of Homeland Security, serving in the administration of President Barack Obama.

Worse, they might be working for a terrorist group, sending vital information to the enemy, helping them to plan and prepare an attack. The president wanted no appeal of a firing decision in the homeland security agency. If they were unable to effectively do their jobs, or if they were found to be agents working for or aiding terrorists, they should lose their jobs immediately, without the right to appeal.

Finally, it was agreed that the FBI and CIA would remain separate and independent. On January 24, 2003, the Department of Homeland Security began operations. It was a new "cabinet-level" agency. The head of the department sits in the presidential Cabinet, the committee of top advisors to the president.

Tom Ridge remained as secretary of the DHS until he resigned in 2004. Following the departure of Tom Ridge, Admiral James Loy filled in as acting secretary of Homeland Security from February 1, 2005, until February 15, 2005, when Michael Chertoff was confirmed and sworn into office. Chertoff had been a federal appellate judge and a top official in the Criminal Division of the U.S. Department of Justice. Currently, Janet Napolitano is the third United States secretary of Homeland Security, serving in the administration of President Barack Obama. She is the fourth person (including acting Secretary Loy) to hold the position, which was created after the 9/11 attack.

2
Tasks of Homeland Security

The Department of Homeland Security includes many different agencies and bureaus. All have something to do with protecting the United States. Some intend to prevent terrorist attacks, while others deal with disasters after they occur.

★ FEMA

The Federal Emergency Management Agency, or FEMA, has the job of coordinating the nation's response to disasters of all kinds. People who work at FEMA prepare for terrorist attacks. They also handle natural disasters, such as earthquakes, floods, fires, tsunamis, volcanoes, blizzards, and landslides.

FEMA agents coordinate rescue efforts after the disaster takes place. They can rush ambulances, helicopters, and rescue dogs to the scene to find survivors. They can set up emergency housing for people who lose their homes.

When the governor of a state declares a state of emergency and requests federal aid, FEMA swings into action. Its people make contact with local "first responders"—the first people to arrive at the scene. FEMA can summon other nearby units for the rescue effort.

FEMA's National Emergency Training Center is an important tool for local emergency managers. The Center runs a number of classes nationwide to prepare Emergency Response teams at all levels. In this photo, Community Emergency Response Team (CERT) leaders are being trained in Emmitsburg, Maryland.

Some natural disasters require days or months of attention. Many people want to volunteer to help. FEMA agents organize these volunteers and send them where they are most needed.

After the attack or disaster, FEMA agents investigate the scene. They try to prevent further problems at the site. A chemical may have spilled, or power lines may have been downed. The agents arrange to have the site cleaned up and made safe again.

FEMA also operates a "disaster school," known as the Emergency Management Institute.[1] At this online school, local emergency management officials learn how to handle disasters when they occur. They also learn how to coordinate their work with that of the federal government.

★ Borders and Coastlines

The biggest job of the Department of Homeland Security is protection. The DHS guards the borders, coastlines, ports, and airports of the United States.

The United States Border Patrol is responsible for land boundaries. The United States has only two—with Mexico and Canada. But both of these borders run for long distances, and much of that distance is wilderness.

Border Patrol agents use planes, cars, and foot patrols to do their job.[2] They watch for people trying to cross into the country illegally. They also watch for people bringing illegal items into the country. These include drugs, certain animals, weapons, explosives, and some kinds of food.

The United States Coast Guard (USCG) has a similar task on the water. USCG boats watch the coastal waters of the United States. They also guard seaports. Coast Guard ships have the right to stop any vessel at sea. They can search

Border Patrol Agents participate in a fast rope exercise as part of BORTAC training.

Airline passengers must pass through security screening check-points prior to boarding their flights.

the vessel and question the people on it. If they suspect that someone is breaking the law, or is about to, they can seize vessels and arrest people.

The busiest entrances to the United States are its airports. The DHS is responsible for the security of air travel. The Transportation Security Administration (TSA) screens passengers and baggage on all flights. TSA agents question travelers about their plans. They also screen luggage to make sure it contains no weapons or explosives.[3]

★ Airport Security

Everyone who takes a plane goes through a TSA checkpoint. But TSA agents also operate in places harder to see. Armed air marshals fly on planes to protect flights. The TSA also runs a Federal Flight Deck Officer Program in which some pilots are allowed to be armed. Bomb-sniffing dogs examine luggage to be loaded on a plane. Agents also carefully check passenger manifests—lists of who is supposed to be on the plane. They compare the names of passengers with a "watch list"—a list of known terrorists and criminals who may be trying to get from one place to another.

The TSA has general managers who work in a certain transportation sector: airlines, cargo, maritime (seagoing), highways, railroads, pipelines, and mass transit. These general managers are experts who know about the risks and threats to these systems. They can take measures to prevent terrorist attacks.

★ Information and Preparation

One of the main tasks of the DHS is to prepare and inform the public. The Homeland Security Advisory plays the most important part in this effort. When a terrorist attack is imminent, the agency will raise the threat level to Red. This occurred for the first time in August 2006, when police in Great Britain discovered a plot to destroy at least ten airplanes en route to the United States. The plotters of the attack had planned to bring explosives on board the airplanes. On the way to the United States, they would blow up the planes in mid-flight.[4]

DHS officials made the Red-level warning very specific. It applied only to flights from Great Britain to the United States. Suddenly, security on these flights became very tight. Passengers were searched one by one. Screeners examined luggage several times.

Within the United States, the threat level became Orange for all aviation. Agents of the TSA met with airport officials to plan new security measures. Passengers would have to go through more careful screening, searches, and interviews. Also, they could not bring any liquids on board: no water, no juice, and especially no shampoo, cans of shaving cream, or hair gel bottles, which can easily hide explosive substances.[5]

The DHS and its agents must think one step ahead of criminals and terrorists. For this reason, DHS officials often change their plans and procedures. Each change is meant to adapt to new threats.

In many ways, the task of the DHS is as important as any in the United States government. A terrorist attack can paralyze the entire nation. It can disrupt cities and harm the national economy for months and years. The terrorist attacks of September 11, 2001, led to the creation of the Department of Homeland Security. Its employees and the agencies that fall under its umbrella must now try to ensure that such an attack does not happen again. It may seem like an impossible task, but the men and women of the department have accepted the challenge.

3

The OSS and the CIA

The time was June 1942. World War II was raging all over the European continent. The armies of Nazi Germany had overrun much of the land and occupied almost all of the European countries. In December 1941, Japan had bombed Pearl Harbor, an important United States military base in Hawaii. Soon, the United States was fighting Japan in the Pacific.

The Army and Navy had their own spy agencies. But these agencies did not work together. They did not coordinate their operations. They jealously guarded any information they had. If one agency broke an enemy code, it did not tell the other.

To help the situation, the Office of Strategic Services (OSS) was formed.[1] The director of the OSS was William "Wild Bill" Donovan. The agency organized and trained underground fighters in Europe and Asia who would fight against or spy on the occupying Japanese and Germans. The OSS also recruited spies in many foreign countries. These spies passed on important information to the OSS agents during the war.

★ The Birth of the CIA

World War II ended in the summer of 1945. In October of that year, the OSS closed down. In William Donovan's view, gathering information and recruiting spies was still a vital task for the United States government. He asked President Harry Truman to continue the agency's work. The president agreed. He ordered the Central Intelligence Group formed in January 1946.

In 1947, the U.S. Congress passed the National Security Act.[2] This law created the modern Central Intelligence Agency, as well as other security agencies. The agency's headquarters was on E Street in Washington, D.C. Its agents would work in foreign countries, collecting information useful to the United States government.

A new law passed in 1949. The Central Intelligence Agency Act allowed the CIA to function in secret. The CIA did not have to make public how it spent its money. It did not have to reveal anything about its operations. There were few controls on what the agency did.

This image was taken from a RF-101 Voodoo spy plane during what is known as the Cuban Missile Crisis. It is a United States Air Force reconnaissance photograph of Soviet missile sites on Cuba.

At the time, the United States and the Soviet Union were fighting the Cold War. The two superpowers were seeking allies all over the world. The United States saw the fight against the Soviet Union and the spread of Communism as the CIA's most important task.

The KGB was the secret intelligence agency of the Soviet Union. The CIA tried to recruit KGB agents to work against their own government. Similarly, the KGB collected information and tried to turn CIA agents into spies for the Soviets.

The CIA also tried to carry out assassination programs. The agency targeted enemies of the United States. One of its targets, Fidel Castro, was the leader of Cuba, a Communist nation in the Caribbean Sea.[3] The agency also helped to overthrow the lawful governments of Chile and Iran.[4] These governments were seen as unfriendly to the United States.

In the 1960s, the United States was fighting against North Vietnamese communists in the Southeast Asian nation of Vietnam. The CIA was an important part of the war. The agency illegally spied on people that were opposed to the war. Most of this work took place in the United States, even though the CIA was supposed to be banned from doing so.

★ CIA Is Scrutinized

In the early 1970s, President Richard Nixon also made use of the CIA. Nixon ordered the agency to spy on his political enemies. In 1973, the Watergate scandal broke out. Nixon decided to resign from office in August 1974. For its role in the affair, the CIA came under fire from the U.S. Congress.

Congress investigated the CIA and held public hearings. In these hearings, many of the CIA's secret doings were made public. Lawmakers put a stop to some of the CIA's operations in the United States and abroad.

Fidel Castro took control of the island nation of Cuba in 1959. In the early 1960s the CIA unsuccessfully plotted to overthrow his regime.

The MQ-1 Predator is an unmanned aircraft, or drone, that has been used by the United States since 1995. This type of aircraft can be used for the purpose of reconnaissance, or as a weapon when armed with two AGM-114 Hellfire missiles.

The CIA had to reveal to Congress how it carried out some of its operations. Also, it could no longer carry out assassinations. Presidents could not use it to help their political careers or help them win elections.

Most countries have intelligence agencies like the CIA. But few investigate them, or hold public hearings on their actions. Few spy agencies have controls, imposed by lawmakers, on what they can do. In his book, *Secrecy and Democracy: The CIA in Transition,* Stansfield Turner, a former head of the CIA, wrote, "Of the world's democracies, only the United States has gone so far to ensure that even this, the most secret arm of government, is responsive to the will of the people."[5]

The CIA must work within limits. There are things it can do, and other things it cannot do, according to federal law. It is the price the agency pays for working within an open and democratic society.

★ The CIA and Terrorism

After the terrorist attacks of September 11, 2001, fighting terrorism became the most important task of the CIA. CIA agents in foreign countries sought information on the whereabouts of terrorists. The CIA sent satellites and drones over the Middle East. The *Predator* drone had no pilot aboard. It held powerful cameras as well as missiles. The mission of the *Predator* was to seek and destroy terrorist leaders and their camps.

The National Counterterrorism Center, or NCTC, coordinates these efforts.[6] Information in many forms arrives at the NCTC. For example, signals intelligence, or sigint, allows CIA analysts to hear conversations picked up from satellite telephones, radio sets, and mobile phones.

★ Functions of the NCTC

The NCTC attempts to understand terrorist groups. The center collects information on their weapons, their members, and their plans. Analysts track the money that funds terrorists in an effort to find out who is supporting them and how the money is sent. The NCTC also works with foreign agencies in countries where terrorists are operating.

The center also tracks terrorist leaders. When one is located, the center may pass the information to the military so that an attack can be carried out. Or, the center will advise the FBI of the suspect's location. Within the United States, the FBI is responsible for nabbing the leader. When the NCTC discovers a threat of terrorism, it warns those responsible for preventing the attack. This includes first responders such as police, paramedics and EMTs, and fire and rescue departments.

★ Threats Around the World

The CIA is vital to the government's response to other threats. Information collected by the CIA allows the president to take action and make decisions. In many dangerous places, this information helps to decide the foreign policy of the United States.

North Korea, for example, is a small nation in eastern Asia that the United States views as a serious threat. The North Korean leadership has built a large army and is attempting to prepare nuclear missiles. The CIA keeps constant watch over North Korean missile sites.[7] CIA analysts can examine intercepted messages sent between North Korean leaders and scientists.

President Barack Obama named General David Petraeus(left), the U.S. head of international forces in Afghanistan, as the new CIA director. Here U.S. Army General David H. Petraeus, former commander of the International Security Assistance Force, speaks with Colonel Massimo Biagini, commander of the Italian Task Force North, in Bala Morghab, Afghanistan in August, 2010.

North Korea's neighbor, the People's Republic of China, also has a nuclear arsenal, albeit a much bigger one. China has large military bases along its seacoasts. Units in the Fujian province are prepared to invade the island of Taiwan.[8] CIA agents on the ground are watching this activity and gathering information. We do not know for sure, but there is a chance they may talk to Chinese soldiers or listen for rumors among civilians. If China decides to attack Taiwan, the CIA hopes to know exactly when and how.

Another dangerous flash point is the subcontinent of South Asia. India and Pakistan are both nuclear-armed nations, and hostile toward each other. The two nations have fought wars and invaded each other's territory. Using satellites and reconnaissance aircraft, the CIA is watching the long border between India and Pakistan. Agents are trying to gather information on army maneuvers in the region. The United States wants to deter a war that could possibly go nuclear.

The most important job in the CIA remains the fight against terrorism. If a terrorist group buys or steals a nuclear weapon, the United States could come under nuclear attack. For this reason, the CIA is watching and listening.

The agency also traces nuclear weapons and nuclear material from the former Soviet Union. It wants to know if North Korea, a country the Soviet Union helped arm, is selling these weapons to terrorist groups. It follows bank transactions, intercepts e-mails, and photographs terrorist training camps. In a very secretive and dangerous world, the CIA provides the leaders of the federal government with information that only spies can gather.

Working for the CIA

About twenty thousand people work for the CIA. Each employee must be an American citizen. They must also go through a tough period of training and education.[1]

The CIA operates a training school at Camp Peary, located near Williamsburg, Virginia. This place is known as "The Farm." At The Farm, future CIA case officers learn important skills. They learn how to follow people, and how to avoid being followed. They learn how to communicate with each other. They also learn how to recruit and command foreign agents.

Many of these undercover agents are part of the National Clandestine Service, a branch of the CIA. These agents often have to work a day job in the area where they are undercover in addition to doing their duties as an agent. This way, they will look less suspicious and less like an outsider.

CIA recruits quickly learn that they must have people skills. They will spend most of their time in contact with people of all kinds. The recruits must learn how to convince others to work for them. In return for information, they will offer something the target may want—money, luxury items, or a chance to leave their own country.

In the words of Lindsay Moran, a former agent who went through the training experience, "Our life's mission was to spot, assess, develop, and recruit foreign spies. These foreign spies—'agents' or 'assets' in CIA lingo—would sell us, their case officers, *secrets*. . . . we were educated on how to spot and befriend anyone who might have access to valuable information."[2]

The career of a CIA case officer depends on this skill. The agency measures success by a simple number. The more agents a case officer can recruit, the more successful his or her career.

★ Recruiting Foreign Agents

CIA case officers work in foreign countries all over the world. Officially, most case officers work for the United States embassy in these countries. But their official job is just part of an elaborate cover story. Their diplomatic status protects them in case they should be caught spying.

Embassy diplomats are immune from arrest and prosecution in foreign countries. If they are caught spying, the host country will simply send them home. They cannot arrest them or put them in jail. They can only be detained while their diplomatic status is being verified.

In the event that an officer is caught and deported, his or her own country may also expel somebody from the host country. The two countries may go on for some time expelling spies. This is known as a "spy war."

The basic and most important job of a case officer is to recruit foreign agents. These agents are usually natives of the host country. They have some job or government position that gives them access to valuable information.

To recruit foreign agents, case officers must first gain a wide circle of friends and associates. He or she must attend parties, social events, public occasions, official meetings, and conferences of all kinds. The officer then must identify a person who may be willing to spy or provide information on his or her own country.

The CIA Wall of Honor is a memorial to all of the fallen CIA agents who have served the agency. The wall is located in the lobby of the CIA headquarters.

The case officer gets acquainted with his target. He gains the target's trust and friendship. He or she also tries to discover the target's personal habits, desires, and weaknesses. At some point, the case officer makes an offer. He or she asks the target to gather information and turn it over to the CIA, usually in exchange for money.

★ Can They Be Trusted?

Secret agents cooperate out of desire for money, for excitement, or out of opposition to their own government. They take a dangerous risk. A case officer may only be expelled for spying.

Getting caught is not good for a CIA case officer's career. But the agent risks much more. If caught, a foreign agent can be arrested, jailed, or executed for cooperating with the CIA.

Not all foreign agents stay loyal to their CIA handlers. Some only pretend to cooperate. In fact, they only pretend to have access to secret information. Or they remain loyal to their host country. They pass information about the CIA and its own agents to their other handlers. They also may pass false information to their CIA handlers.

These "double agents" can disrupt and destroy the work of CIA case officers. That is why a case officer must be an excellent judge of a person's character and motivation.

★ Running Secret Agents

When a foreign agent agrees to cooperate, the CIA case officer sets up a way for the two to communicate. They cannot use phones or e-mail, which can be intercepted. The agent must find a safer way to send information— in the form of documents or photographs—to his handler. The handler must convey secret instructions to the agent.

There are many different ways to carry this out. The two may pass the documents directly to each other while meeting in public. They may exchange envelopes, briefcases, or shopping bags. The best place to do so is at a public park, a sports stadium, or a crowded public marketplace. The crowd of people makes it harder for the police or enemy spies to follow them.

Or they may use a "dead drop." The handler and the agent arrange for an exchange of information without actually meeting. The person passing the document places it in a container. He leaves the container in a hiding place.[3]

The drop site must be easy to view from a distance. The receiver surveys the site, looking for anyone who might be watching. If the coast is clear, he or she then picks up the document and quickly leaves.

★ Spycraft

The foreign agent's job is to collect information and keep it secret. He gets support from the CIA's Directorate of Science and Technology.[4] This department is responsible for creating technology to support intelligence-gathering missions. The directorate provides cameras, computers, listening devices, and communications systems to agents and case officers all over the world.

To gather information, the agent can take photographs with tiny cameras. Agents have fitted these cameras in their eyeglasses, in pen caps, and in the buttons on their overcoats. They have also used powerful long-distance listening devices to record conversations.

CIA agents may decide to "bug" a room. They plant listening devices in the room. The tiny devices nest within light fixtures, smoke detectors, office equipment, potted plants, or wall hangings. The listening devices can also be placed in their shoes, their belts, their wallets—anywhere in their clothing or on their person.

There are hundreds of other ways to collect information. Some of them are very simple and have been used for centuries. One device opens letters without damaging the envelope. Others methods are more high tech. Computer programs can allow the CIA to hack into a foreign government's secret communications and e-mail.

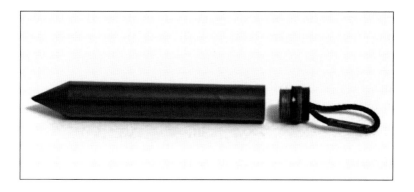

The dead drop spike is a device that allows CIA agents to conceal money, maps, documents, film or other items. In use since the late 1960s, it is waterproof and mildew-proof and can be placed in the ground or a shallow body of water to be retrieved later.

★ A Clandestine Force

Information stays secret. Agents only know the people they need to know. The CIA wants them to know nothing of what other agents are doing. CIA case officers, even those working in the same country, only know the agents they are handling. Only top officials at headquarters know everything the CIA is doing in a single country.

In 1961, the CIA headquarters moved from Washington, D.C., to a newer, larger complex in Langley, Virginia. Headquarters remains a secret to the outside world. At the Langley complex, a separate building is used for meetings and to greet guests. In the main headquarters building, there are no visitors allowed at any time. Security officers patrol the halls. The Technical Security Division examines each room for bugs, or listening devices.

"White noise" machines create a steady, low-level hum. The hum makes it difficult for any undetected bugs to pick up quiet conversations. Computerized locks prevent the workers from wandering into areas where they do not belong.[5]

★ Analyzing Top Secret Information

The CIA analyzes information that it gathers within the Directorate of Intelligence (DOI). The CIA has thousands of DOI analysts working at Langley. Each has responsibility for a specific country or area of the world.

CIA analysts must be experts in the culture, geography, government, and armed forces of a foreign country. They

This lighter concealing a small camera is only one type of device that may be used by a CIA agent or case officer to gather information.

must know how well its economy is doing. They must know how to speak its language. They should know how big its army and navy are, and how many ships, tanks, and military planes the country owns.

Analysts have many sources of information. They can use satellite pictures from the National Reconnaissance Office (NRO) and electronic messages intercepted by the National Security Agency (NSA). They have reports from CIA case officers working abroad. They may have photographs taken by surveillance aircraft. They may also have information from the armed forces or the Department of State.

The analyst spends his or her day reading, looking at images, writing reports, and communicating with superiors. He or she must take all the information provided by foreign agents. The information may be incomplete or inaccurate. It may be a pack of lies provided by a double agent.

The analyst has to decide. His or her report helps the rest of the government—the president, the military, diplomats, and CIA officials—decide how to proceed. In many cases, this information has helped top government officials make important decisions on foreign policy. Analysts' reports may help to prevent terrorist attacks, or start wars in foreign countries.

★ The Director

The Director of the Central Intelligence Agency, or DCIA, is at the head of the CIA. He works with the Director of National Intelligence (DNI) to help the DNI collect information from all departments of the government, not just the CIA. The DNI advises the president on matters and important news. When a crisis arises overseas, the president relies on the DNI to keep him informed.

Modern day CIA Headquarters in Langley, Virginia. As the CIA has grown over the years, so has the building. The original design actually included open space with the anticipation that the organization would expand over the years and require additional building and parking. The building has stood the same since 1991.

The president himself appoints the DCIA and the DNI. Before he or she can take this post, the candidate must go before the Senate to answer questions. The director candidate has to explain how the CIA will operate under its new director.

It is a complex job. There is a lot of competition within the federal government. Other spy agencies jealously guard their information. The military, for example, spies on armed forces around the world. But it does not want to reveal what it knows to the CIA or anyone else. It does not want to give up control of its operations to civilians.

Coordination is extremely important. This is especially true in the age of terrorism. If a military spy learns of a terrorist threat, the CIA and other federal agencies should know as well. Information sharing is crucial in stopping a terrorist attack. In this task, it is the director's responsibility to see that the CIA gets, and gives, all the needed information.

At the same time, presidents shy away from giving the DCIA too much power. In the words of Stansfield Turner:

> They do not want any one person to have full control over the way in which special information . . . is employed . . . the record of the CIA, the NSA, and Army intelligence in poking into American lives in the 1950s and 1960s cannot be ignored. If some DCI did abuse the combined powers of those agencies, it could cause untold damage to our citizens—and to our intelligence.[6]

The CIA must make a careful balance; it must collect and analyze information, but it must also follow federal law. Those who spy for the United States know their actions can have serious consequences. It makes working for the agency a tough, complex, dangerous, yet very interesting job.

5

The National Security Agency

There are a number of intelligence agencies (at least sixteen) in the United States government. Each branch of the military collects and analyzes intelligence. The CIA spies all over the world. But the National Security Agency is the largest such agency. It is also the most secretive. That is why some people joke that the initials NSA stand for "No Such Agency."

The NSA was established on November 4, 1952, in an executive order written by President Harry Truman.[1] Its mission is to collect communications in any form. It eavesdrops on electronic signals of all kinds, and it protects the top-secret communications of the United States government.

NSA antennae and listening devices intercept any and all forms of communications. This includes radio broadcasting, Internet communications (including e-mail), microwave and satellite transmissions, telephone calls—anything with an electronic signal.

★ History of the NSA

Like the CIA, the NSA has its roots in World War II. In September 1939, war broke out in Europe. Germany attacked Poland, its eastern neighbor. In the next year, German armies swept across Western Europe. German bombers attacked London and other British cities from the air.

Harry S. Truman was the thirty-third president of the United States. Truman created the National Security Agency (NSA) by issuing an executive order in 1952.

The British intercepted German messages, but the messages were sent in code. The Germans were using an encryption machine known as Enigma. The machine used rotors and electrical circuits to substitute one letter for another.

British mathematicians, including Alan Turing, cracked the Enigma codes.[2] That allowed them to read Germany's top secret messages and war plans. British leaders knew about enemy troop movements and the position of German ships and submarines at sea.

The British knew this intercepted intelligence as Ultra, and kept it top secret. Ultra messages helped the Allies (the United States, Great Britain, and others) end the war in 1945.

Britain shared this information with the United States. United States code breakers were also hard at work. In Asia, Japan was using another cipher machine known as Purple. This code was cracked by cryptographers even before the Japanese attack on Pearl Harbor.[3] But the attack still came as a surprise because Purple was used for diplomatic codes. Japan did not send any messages about military plans using the Purple system.

In the United States, cryptographers knew the decoded Japanese messages as Magic. The intercepted Magic messages allowed them to follow the plans of Japanese leaders and diplomats. But the code breakers did not always share Magic messages with the people who needed them. Magic messages were top secret, and those responsible for protecting Pearl Harbor did not receive them. Better coordination may have allowed the military to prepare for the attack, which killed almost 2,500 people.

★ Armed Forces Security Agency

The United States was successful at cracking several other enemy codes. The government and the military employed expert code breakers to listen in and interpret these

The Enigma cipher machine. The Germans used this encoding instrument for sending secret messages during World War II. While it seemed nearly impossible to break the machine's coding system—there were 150,000,000,000,000,000,000 possibilities—the Allies were eventually able to crack its codes.

communications. In 1949, four years after the end of the war, the Armed Forces Security Agency (AFSA) was established.[4] The agency was responsible for communications sent to, or received by, the intelligence branches of the armed forces—the Army, the Navy, the Air Force and the Marine Corps.

The Armed Forces Security Agency had difficulty coordinating its work. Although the war was over, the country still needed to intercept and analyze communications. The Cold War had broken out. The United States and the Soviet Union were rivals. In 1950, the Korean War began. The U. S. military fought alongside the South Koreans against North Korea and Communist China, both allies of the Soviet Union.

A better way of collecting electronic communication was necessary. As a result, the government established the NSA in 1952. The NSA's work extended beyond the military to include all branches of the federal government.

★ ECHELON

The NSA coordinated its activities with other intelligence agencies in much of the English-speaking world—in Canada, Great Britain, Australia, and New Zealand. This became known as the UKUSA Group.

In the 1960s, the nations of the UKUSA worked together to plot against the Soviet Union. The group needed a way to share information. For this reason, the members of the group created the ECHELON system.[5]

ECHELON allowed the NSA and the UKUSA group to intercept voice, electronic communications, radio, and satellite transmissions. Later, the system intercepted telex, faxes, and Internet traffic. In the 1960s and 1970s, ECHELON spied on Soviet military signals. It intercepted messages from Soviet ships at sea, and from Soviet tank and infantry units on the ground. It also spied on Soviet diplomats in cities around the world.

In 1991, the Soviet Union collapsed. The Communist threat receded from Europe and the rest of the world. ECHELON was given new assignments. It spied on drug dealers and terrorists. One of its most important functions was to listen to satellite phone calls.

Each member of the UKUSA group was assigned a specific area of the world to watch. Canada listens to Russia and to foreign embassies around the world. The United States and the NSA monitor Latin America and eastern Asia. The British are responsible for Europe and Africa, and Australia keeps an eye on southern Asia. New Zealand monitors the vast distances and scattered islands of the Pacific Ocean.

Some countries outside the UKUSA alliance are unhappy with the ECHELON system. They are suspicious of the work of the NSA and its sister agencies. They believe that the NSA may be spying on their citizens and their businesses. It is believed that the NSA may be trying to learn closely kept industrial trade secrets, such as secret manufacturing processes. It can pass these secrets on to private companies within the United States.

The NSA denies it is doing this kind of work. It claims that it takes interest only in messages that affect the national security of the United States. But many people guard their communications anyway. They use computer programs to encrypt their e-mails and other transmissions. The NSA works hard to crack these codes.

★ Listening Posts

The NSA can intercept messages anywhere in the world. Its analysts divide these intercepts into signals intelligence (sigint) and electronic intelligence (elint). The agency has listening posts on mountaintops, in barren deserts, on islands at sea, and in the frozen wastes of the Arctic Sea.

The NSA has important listening posts at Menwith Hill in Yorkshire, England. For traffic in the United States, NSA has posts at Yakima, Washington, and Sugar Grove, West Virginia.

These posts have powerful antennae that can detect any kind of electronic signal that is moving through the air. All of this intercepted message traffic flows to NSA headquarters at Fort Meade, Maryland.

One thing the NSA cannot do is spy on United States citizens within the United States. A law known as Signals Intelligence Directive 18 prohibits this activity.[6] To monitor United States citizens, the agency needs a warrant issued by a court that has found probable cause to authorize such spying. Special secret courts meet to issue these warrants, or to deny them.

In 2002, President George W. Bush, in an executive order, allowed the NSA to eavesdrop on United States citizens who the agency believes are contacting known terrorists. The NSA will not need a warrant in the event that it suspects the person is involved in terrorism. It can collect data from e-mails and wiretaps on private telephone calls.

The NSA may also spy on citizens when they are in a foreign country speaking with foreign citizens. Author James Bamford relates that:

> Unlike information on United States persons, which cannot be kept longer than a year, information on foreign citizens can be held eternally. As permanent as India ink, the mark may remain with the person forever. He will never be told how he was placed on a customs blacklist, who put him there, why he lost a contract—or worse.[7]

The NSA has a huge computer storage system. It has trillions of pages of data. It has many supercomputers and specialized computer systems of its own. It hires contractors to design and maintain these systems.

★ At NSA Headquarters

The budget of the National Security Agency is kept secret. In addition, no one is sure exactly how many people work for the NSA.

The NSA has a huge job. It collects electronic information in any form. Every day, it intercepts millions of mobile phone and satellite telephone calls, e-mails, and other forms of electronic communication. If communication is sent in code, the NSA has the job of breaking the code and translating the message.

The NSA relies on the fact that many telephone calls move from place to place through the air. Cell phone calls, for example, are relayed via microwave towers. The calls can be intercepted with the right equipment.

Most of these messages have nothing to do with security or terrorism. In order to find important information, the NSA needs thousands of people to run its computers. It also needs a way to filter out ordinary messages. That is the most important job of the analysts working at Fort Meade.

6

Intercepts and Analysis

Each analyst at the NSA has a specialty. The specialty may be a certain language—Thai or Chinese or Russian.[1] Other analysts may specialize in certain military weapons, such as jet fighters, tanks, or missiles. There are NSA analysts who specialize in economics, in media, in transportation, and in computer systems.

At his or her desk, the analyst receives intercepts of communications captured by NSA satellites or listening devices. The intercepts have been decoded, if necessary. The analyst translates the intercept into English. In many cases, the intercepts have no importance. They are just ordinary conversations or messages. They have no effect on United States security.

In other cases, the messages are very important. They may reveal a secret arms deal or the military plan of a foreign government. The information may be vital to an arm of the United States government. Many federal agencies are "customers" of the NSA. They have asked the agency for reports on people, places, or events they need to know about.

If the intercept holds any importance, the analyst writes a detailed report. The report summarizes the intercept and explains what it means. The report is coded according to how secret it must remain. There are other codes that show how the intercept was received, and what its subject is.

The analyst then sends the report to the "customer"—the agency of the federal government that has asked for the information. The customer could be the CIA, the Department of State, the U.S. Army or Navy, or the White House. There are many federal agencies that have the right to ask for NSA information or assistance.

The NSA only sends reports and summaries to its customers. It never sends the intercepts or any raw data. These are absolutely secret and are kept within the NSA buildings at Fort Meade. Only a very few people ever see them. The computers that display the intercepts have no Internet connection. Nobody from outside the NSA can read them.[2]

★ A Vital Information System

The NSA analyst has access to a very powerful computer system from a simple, ordinary office desktop. The NSA "Intranet" is a closed system, available only to people working within the agency. The system works through a search engine. By entering certain keywords, the analyst can pull up reports from the past concerning a certain subject.

He or she can also use coded abbreviations. NSA analysts have tagged their reports with these codes according to their subject matter. Entering the abbreviation calls up all the past reports on that particular subject, but never the intercept itself.

The intercept is top secret, even within the NSA. Translating it is the job of people working apart from the analysts. The analysts can only make a written report on the intercept—they cannot relay the text.

The NSA uses keywords for intercepting communications. There are billions of phone calls and e-mail messages sent every day, all over the world. The NSA computers are searching these communications for certain words or names.

When any of those names or words are used in an e-mail, for example, the NSA computer tags the message. Any e-mail with a wanted terrorist such as "Osama bin Laden" in its subject line, for example, is likely to be intercepted and downloaded by the NSA. The e-mail is translated if necessary. If the analyst finds vital information within the e-mail, he or she will summarize it in a report and send it to an NSA customer—perhaps the FBI.

The FBI and other law-enforcement agencies rely on NSA reports to find and track criminal suspects. They can also use the agency to monitor anyone associated with these suspects. Certain groups can be targeted as well. The goal is to know everything that certain people are saying to each other, and in this way, to prevent criminal activity.

★ On the NSA Campus

The NSA headquarters at Fort Meade is a city in itself— "Crypto City," as employees call it. There are 50 buildings in Crypto City, 325 acres of land, and 17,000 parking spaces. About forty thousand people work there—more than all the employees of the CIA and FBI combined.

All of the NSA's operations are top secret and off-limits to the public. The NSA protects its campus with barbed-wire fences, guardhouses, a large police force, and bomb-sniffing dogs. There is only one road leading to NSA headquarters. It is carefully guarded against any trespass by outsiders.

Within Crypto City, employees have many conveniences available to them. There are grocery stores, drugstores, fitness centers, day-care centers, softball fields, and movie theaters. There are hundreds of social clubs for those interested in music, theater, video games, yachting, travel, or Bible study.[3]

To prevent anyone from spying on the NSA, the buildings are protected with layers of copper sheets. The copper prevents electronic signals from escaping the buildings where computers and communications equipment are working.

Each employee wears a plastic badge around his or her neck. The badge must be on display at all times. The badge carries a photograph of the employee. The color, design, and letters on the badge show the employee's security clearance.

Armed guards check the badges of everyone as they pass through security checkpoints. Visitors wear a badge with a large black "V" and must always walk with someone with an "E"—meaning "escort"—badge.

A blue badge means the employee has won top secret clearance. He or she can read very sensitive reports and deal with top secret intercept systems. But to win a blue badge, an NSA employee must pass a series of tough examinations. There is a background check, a polygraph (lie-detector) test, and a detailed briefing. At any time, the privilege of wearing a blue badge can be taken away.

★ Careers at the NSA

The National Security Agency has hundreds of different jobs. Some of them require years of experience and technical expertise. Others require only a good knowledge of a foreign language.[4]

A language or voice analyst translates and analyzes documents. The NSA has trained analysts in about one hundred

An aerial view of the National Security Agency headquarters at Fort Meade, Maryland. Although the number of agency employees is unknown, one clue into its size and operations can be found by the amount of electricity it uses.

Part of the "Purple" Type B Cipher Switch that was used by the Japanese before and during WWII. United States cryptanalysts gave it the codename "Purple" because all work to crack its code was kept in purple colored binders.

different languages, as well as about a dozen different dialects of Arabic. While many people study French or Spanish in high school, other languages are much less commonly known in the United States.

A voice analyst able to listen to and understand a conversation in Icelandic or Pashto, for example, is valuable to the NSA. Language analysts at the agency are also fluent in dialects such as Xhosa, Uzbek, Lingala, Papiamento, Kazakh, Berber, Basque, Amharic, and Ilocano.

Cryptologic linguists apply their knowledge of linguistics to cryptology. They have a deep knowledge of the grammar, syntax, and vocabulary of certain languages. They use these patterns to understand coded messages.

A signals analyst tries to understand how and why a certain source is using electronic communications. The pattern of the signals gives important clues to the kind of equipment the source is using, and helps other analysts to break codes.

There are several different kinds of signals analysts working at the NSA. Morse code collectors only deal with communications using Morse or other codes. Multimode collectors handle electromagnetic signals, such as those sent by telephone or microwave.

There are computer analysts, mathematicians, software engineers, and Infosec (information security) experts. These men and women help develop codes for use by the United States government. There are also polygraph experts, people who help develop and use lie-detection equipment. The NSA is very careful about security—both within the agency and for the federal government as a whole.

7

The History of the FBI

It was a hot summer night on July 22, 1934, at Chicago's Biograph Theater. The movie *Manhattan Melodrama* was letting out. People were strolling from the theater doors onto the sidewalk. Among them was perhaps the most infamous gangster in the nation: John Dillinger.[1]

Men from the Bureau of Investigation were in place. They had the theater surrounded. The "G-Men" (short for "government men") called out to Dillinger. Instead of surrendering, he took flight up a dark alley. Dillinger fell in a hail of bullets. The G-Men had gotten their man. It was an important day for the Bureau of Investigation and the nation's "top cop," J. Edgar Hoover.

★ The Red Scare and "Palmer Raids"

Hoover had been head of the bureau for more than ten years. He made his reputation after World War I, which ended in 1918. He had a talent for collecting information. He was building the bureau into the nation's biggest and best law enforcement agency.

In the years that followed World War I, a Red Scare hit the United States. A revolution in Russia, led by "Reds" (Communists), frightened many people. They believed another revolution could happen in the United States.

J. Edgar Hoover was the first director of the Federal Bureau of Investigation. Appointed director of the Bureau of Investigation—predecessor to the FBI—in 1924, he was instrumental in founding the FBI in 1935, where he remained director until his death in 1972.

Many people were suspected as "Reds." Some of the suspects were labor leaders trying to organize unions. Others were immigrants from southern Europe. Very few were, in fact, Communists.

On one evening in June 1919, bombs arrived at the homes of government leaders and businessmen. One of the bombs exploded on the doorstep of Attorney General A. Mitchell Palmer.[2]

The frightened Palmer ordered a national sweep. Police and agents from the Department of Justice arrested hundreds of people. During the "Palmer Raids," the police threw these suspects in jail without charging them with a crime. They prepared to deport them from the United States.

★ Hoover Takes Charge

Palmer needed information to help this effort. He needed names, addresses, and evidence to use against the suspected Reds. To collect that information, he set up the General Intelligence Division, or GID. The GID was a part of the Department of Justice.

Palmer named J. Edgar Hoover as the first director of the GID. Hoover was working inside the Bureau of Investigation (BOI), a small federal police force that was founded in 1908.[3] The BOI investigated "white collar" crimes. These included fraud, forgery, and embezzlement.

Many government officials and ordinary citizens opposed the Palmer Raids. They did not think it was fair to arrest people without charging them with a crime. They opposed forcing these people out of the country.

The Red Scare died down. Attorney General Palmer predicted a revolution on May Day 1920. The prediction failed to come true. But Hoover and the GID survived. Meanwhile, Hoover had collected an enormous amount of information.

During the administration of President Warren Harding, who served from 1921 to 1923, Hoover became assistant chief of the BOI. He helped the bureau's chief,

Stanley W. Finch was the first to strongly call for the creation of an investigative squad within the U.S. Department of Justice. When a Special Agent force was established in 1908, later called the Bureau of Investigation (BOI), Mr. Finch was assigned its director.

William J. Burns, to collect information to use against Harding's political enemies.[4] After the death of Harding in the summer of 1923, Burns was fired from his job.

J. Edgar Hoover was named the new chief of the BOI on May 10, 1924. He promised to run a professional organization. "Special agents" were hired for their professionalism, neatness, and attention to detail. The BOI was successful in catching many gangsters and ordinary criminals.

The agency earned a better reputation under Hoover's leadership. In 1932, the bureau established its Scientific Crime Detection Laboratory. This became the most up-to-date crime lab in the world. It used modern techniques of criminal investigation, including handwriting analysis and fingerprinting.

★ The Modern FBI

On the morning of June 17, 1933, three gangsters gathered near the entrance to Union Station in Kansas City, Missouri. Vernon Miller, Adam Richetti, and Charles "Pretty Boy" Floyd meant to free their comrade, Frank Nash, from the police. Nash had escaped from Leavenworth Prison. Police had captured him and were bringing him by train back to Kansas City.

The gangsters spotted Nash in custody of Bureau of Investigation agents. They opened fire, killing three Kansas City policemen and two BOI agents. Nash also died in the shoot-out.[5]

The "Kansas City Massacre" inspired J. Edgar Hoover to declare a national "war on crime." The federal government passed new laws to help. Kidnapping, bank robbery, and transportation of stolen property across state lines became federal crimes. The BOI had the authority to investigate them. In 1935, the bureau was renamed the Federal Bureau of Investigation, or FBI.

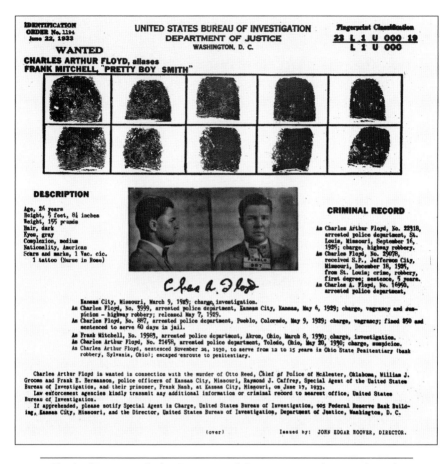

Charles "Pretty Boy" Floyd was one of the most wanted criminals in the history of the FBI.

★ New Methods

The FBI and its G-men fought a crime wave that took place during the Great Depression of the 1930s. The FBI used old and new techniques for investigation. They used room bugs, break-ins, wiretaps on telephones, and the interception of mail and telegrams.

The FBI used these methods despite the fact that they were illegal without gaining the permission of the target. Then, in

1940, President Franklin Roosevelt made such covert (hidden) surveillance legal.[6] World War II was under way in Europe, and Roosevelt believed it was necessary in a time of war.

During World War II, Hoover ran a domestic spy ring that kept tabs on suspected German and Japanese sympathizers. These were people who lived in America and were believed to support the war efforts of those countries. FBI spies worked in factories and within the military. The FBI was also responsible for wartime media censorship.

In 1949, Hoover began the "Ten Most Wanted" list. This is one of the most effective tools the FBI has for catching dangerous criminals. The list allows the public to assist in catching criminals. The FBI "Ten Most Wanted" list is still in effect, with Semion Mogilevich among the criminals on the list. He is wanted for fraud by wire, RICO conspiracy, mail fraud and money laundering among other crimes. [7]

Osama bin Laden, then head of the Islamist militant group al-Qaeda, lead the list until he was killed in Pakistan on Monday, May 2, 2011, by a United States special operations military unit. The operation, code-named Operation Neptune Spear, was ordered by United States President Barack Obama and carried out in a U.S. Central Intelligence Agency (CIA) operation by a team of United States Navy SEALs from the United State Naval Special Warfare Development Group of the Joint Special Operations Command, with support from CIA operatives on the ground.

★ Counterterrorism

The FBI now has the authority to investigate more than two hundred different federal crimes. But its top priority is counterterrorism. The USA Patriot Act, passed in 2002, allows the FBI to use new methods of investigation against terror plots.[8]

FBI agents can track suspects in the United States and abroad. For this task, they have the help of the National Security Agency. NSA super computers and satellites can intercept electronic signals—e-mails, telephone calls, and radio transmissions. NSA analysts can also translate and report on these messages. This information is available to "customers" within the government, including the FBI.

The FBI can also conduct searches. If it suspects someone is involved with a terrorist plot, the FBI must request a court warrant. If the FBI persuades the judge that there is good reason to suspect that someone is involved in a terrorist plot, a judge will issue a search warrant. The warrant allows agents to enter and search a private home. Agents will look for weapons, explosives, mobile telephones, and computers. They will also search for audio tapes, videotapes, computer disks, notebooks, letters, diaries, and tape recorders. Based on what they find, they may make an arrest.

The agents may arrest someone on suspicion of terrorist activity. Or, they may bring in a "material witness." Such a witness, though not a suspect him or herself, may have useful information about criminal suspects.

The FBI coordinates its efforts with other federal agencies, including the CIA and the Department of Defense. Under the USA Patriot Act, these agencies are supposed to share valuable information. This will give FBI agents a clear picture of what other investigators know and are doing.

The 9/11 attacks changed the priorities of the FBI, as well as the CIA and the NSA. The FBI has assigned about half of all its special agents to the fight against terrorism. The directors of the CIA and FBI report to the president nearly every day on the subject. To carry out this assignment, the bureau has many new weapons in its crime-fighting arsenal.

8

How the FBI Works

Along Pennsylvania Ave. in Washington, D.C., stands the massive J. Edgar Hoover Building. Thousands of people come to work in this building every day. At headquarters, the FBI collects information from around the world. Top FBI officials oversee the most important cases.

Security is tight at headquarters. Combination locks protect corridors and entire wings of the building. To pass through some barriers, agents must use a retinal or fingerprint scanner. The scanner compares the pattern of blood vessels in their eyes or their fingerprints to identify them.

Analysts at the bureau collect and use information in many different ways. They track suspected criminals. They build "profiles" of suspects in new crimes. A profile shows the suspect's age, physical appearance, manners, and way of thinking. The profile helps the FBI to find and arrest the suspect.

The FBI also collects information in the fight against terrorism. Analysts send the information to the Department of Homeland Security and the Central Intelligence Agency. FBI agents also track down foreign spies working to gather information inside the United States.

The bureau also deals with cases involving the production or transport of illicit drugs. FBI agents track drug shipments and arrest smugglers and dealers. Violent crimes, white-collar crimes, organized criminal gangs, and foreign spies working in the United States also get the bureau's attention.

The imposing J. Edgar Hoover FBI Building on Pennsylvania Avenue in Washington, D.C., was officially dedicated by President Gerald R. Ford in 1975. Its 2.8 million square feet of floor space houses more than seven thousand employees.

FBI agent in training.

★ Training

Bureau agents begin their careers at the FBI Academy in Quantico, Virginia. The FBI Academy was built on the grounds of the U.S. Marine Corps Camp Quantico base, south of Washington, D.C. The FBI began operating out of the current structure in May 1972.[1]

The FBI will not say how long the training period lasts, but it is believed to be between sixteen and twenty-one weeks. In that time, people, some with little or no law-enforcement experience, become FBI agents. They prepare to investigate the most serious crimes, learn how to wear disguises, and work undercover. They become better at handling and shooting firearms. They also learn the many rules and regulations an FBI agent needs to know.

A big part of training is preparing for difficult and dangerous situations. Agents practice encounters with criminals and witnesses. They also learn what to do when they reach the scene of a crime.

The academy has everything an average college campus has. It has a swimming pool, a gym, a cafeteria where the food is free, a laundry, and a store.

To apply for a job with the FBI, a United States citizen must be between the ages of twenty-three and thirty-seven. They must have a four-year college degree. They also have to go through a background check, which will discover if they have ever been convicted of a serious crime.

Competition is tough. As many as fifteen thousand people take the FBI entrance examination each year, but only about five hundred are accepted. The FBI wants people who are totally dedicated to the job. One FBI official, Lawrence A. Bonney, put it like this:

> If you're here . . . to stay three or four years and go out and get yourself a high-paying job, with a little moniker at the end that says 'former FBI agent,' don't

waste our time, don't waste your time. We want folks who are committed to the United States of America and believe in what it stands for, and in its ideals. We want people who will make a difference, who have a sense of mission, and we want people who believe in truth, justice, and the American way, as hokey as that sounds.[2]

★ In the Field

The FBI runs fifty-six field offices. These are local offices where agents handle cases, collect information, and track suspects. The agents work with local police to solve serious crimes that take place in the area. A Special Agent in Charge (SAC) runs each field office.

Each field office has a communications room, where technicians operate telephones and video monitors. Each has a weapons vault, where shotguns, machine guns, body armor, and ammunition are kept. Each has an office for a SWAT (special weapons and tactics) team. There is a surveillance office that manages all suspect-tracking.

Downstairs is the garage for bureau cars. The "bucars" are unmarked vehicles. They are large, four-door cars with high-horsepower engines. Inside, the cars have cell phones, public-address systems, two-way encrypted radios, and a rack for shotguns.

★ Offices Home and Abroad

In addition to the field offices, there are about four hundred smaller FBI offices known as resident agencies. Some of them are very small. A resident agency may have only one FBI agent. But all resident agencies serve an important purpose.

FBI intelligence analyst JD Narula spoke recently at an FBI Community Relations Executive Seminar Training (CREST) event held at a Sikh temple in New Jersey. More than 55 youth and 10 temple leaders attended the event, which included presentations on FBI operations, hate crimes, recruitment, the Evidence Response Team, K-9 units, counterintelligence, and agent self-defense tactics.

The resident agencies investigate crimes in smaller communities. They work with local police officers. They are often the first to reach the scene of an important crime that will become an FBI case.

Every square mile of the United States has at least one FBI agent assigned to cover it. The resident agents report to their nearest field office. The SAC at the field office gives them instructions and orders.

The FBI also has offices in foreign countries. These Legal Attaches, or "Legats," investigate crimes against the United States. They coordinate investigation work with local police. They also track suspected terrorists.

Members of the FBI SWAT teams are sometimes in great danger.

A Special Agent in Charge oversees each field office, except for the largest field offices, in Washington, D.C., Los Angeles, and New York City. These large offices are under the control of an assistant director.

The SAC assigns cases to the special agents. The special agent, and one or several partners, is responsible for the investigation of the case. He or she looks for clues, tracks down leads, and works with local law enforcement to catch and arrest criminals.

Ronald Kessler, in his book *The FBI*, reports that SAC is the job FBI agents aspire to: "Most agents consider special agent in charge to be the best job in the FBI because an SAC is totally responsible for the work produced in his area and does not report on a daily basis to anyone."[3]

★ Priority Cases

In the past, FBI agents investigated as many crimes as possible. Under J. Edgar Hoover, the bureau sought to rack up as many solved cases as possible. Agents worked many cases at once—sometimes as many as fifty at a time.

After Hoover died in 1972, things changed. FBI agents started working on "priority cases." These were cases involving criminal gangs and conspiracies. They worked a case for a long period of time, sometimes years. They paid informants to pass along information. They sometimes allowed small-time criminals to continue their work—in the hope they would catch a major gang leader or drug dealer.

The agents may have done very little work on each case. But good statistics were important. Hoover wanted Congress to see a higher number of solved cases every year. The lawmakers would then give the bureau a larger budget every year.

A variety of "spy gear" tools used by undercover FBI agents may include false passports, guns and ammunition, a cell phone, camera, a wristwatch with hidden listening device or built-in camera, and money (including foreign currency).

An FBI Evidence Response Team is shown learning skills to aid them in their work. They are at work learning how to recover evidence at the scene of a crime.

The FBI has many techniques of investigation to use in priority cases. They take photographs. They carry out surveillance from cars, trucks, vans, airplanes, rooftops, and adjoining rooms. They record phone conversations, open mail, and bug rooms. They follow suspects on foot or in their bucars. They look for evidence of crime or a conspiracy to commit a crime.

This kind of work sometimes puts FBI agents in great danger. In some cases, the agent may have to go undercover. He assumes a disguise to move in the same circles as the suspect. He or she may take a job in a store or restaurant to follow a suspect on a daily basis. Or, the FBI may start up a "front" company. Acting as a real business, the FBI "front" may fool the suspect into revealing an act of fraud or theft.

When they go undercover, agents wear a disguise. They also sometimes have to wear secret recording devices. They have to blend in with criminals and be accepted by them. They spend weeks or months acting their role. All the time, their lives are at risk, and agents are occasionally killed in the line of duty.

★ Discipline

The bureau has a lot of rules for agents to follow. In the past, under J. Edgar Hoover, these rules reached down to the smallest details of private life. FBI agents had to wear white shirts, ties, and polished black shoes. They could not have beards or mustaches. They could not drink coffee during working hours because the bureau did not want them wasting time on coffee breaks. They also had to wear hats—even after hats went out of style.

Much of this changed after the death of J. Edgar Hoover in 1972. The FBI entered a new era. Rules of conduct and dress relaxed, as they did in American society. But the FBI still keeps a close watch on agents and what they do. The Inspection Division and the Office of Professional Responsibility (OPR) are responsible for this task.

When someone accuses an agent of improper conduct, the Inspection Division takes over the case. An agent may have falsified documents or lied to his SAC. He may have used bureau money or employees for personal reasons. He may have given out the name of an FBI informant or undercover agent. He may have taken drugs or accepted a bribe from a suspect.

The Inspection Division gathers all the facts relevant to the case. It interviews anyone who may know anything about it. It also gives the agent under investigation a polygraph (lie detector) test.

The polygraph is one of the most important tools in the FBI. It measures a person's breathing, heart rate, blood pressure, and other physical signs. It uses these signs to help determine if a person is lying about a crime or about misconduct.

The polygraph operator sits the suspect down and attaches electrodes to his or her body. The FBI inspector then asks a series of "control" questions. These simple queries deal with a person's name, age, birth date, address— the basic facts of his or her life. The control questions are meant to measure the person's normal physical responses to questioning. Tougher questions follow, usually about secrets in the person's personal life. The polygraph now shows the operator how that person reacts when lying, making explanations or excuses, or evading questions.

Then questions involving the crime or misconduct are asked. The suspect will answer truthfully or not. If the polygraph shows no change in physical stress, then the suspect has "passed." If there are changes—faster breathing and heart rate, for example—then the suspect has "failed."

The polygraph does not prove anything—results cannot be used in court because they are not considered to be reliable enough. Polygraph results, however, do help investigators decide whether or not to drop a case.

★ Offices of the FBI

The Strategic Information and Operations Center (SIOC) is the nerve center of the FBI during a crisis. When a major event occurs, such as a terrorist attack, the SIOC swings into action.[4]

The center covers a huge room within FBI headquarters. Computer monitors line dozens of long desks. The SIOC buzzes with activity. FBI men and women give out instructions to the field offices. They monitor telephones, video screens, and the Internet. They coordinate rescue efforts, the hunt for suspects, and the work of local police officers. They also coordinate any FBI work with the military and other government agencies.

When the crisis is over, the FBI remains involved. An Office of Victim Assistance (OVA) helps people who have lost their homes or loved ones.[5] The OVA keeps people informed of how the FBI is working on the case. It helps them find counseling and shelter, if necessary.

It also keeps the victim of a crime informed about the suspect. When the suspect goes on trial, the victim knows about it. Through the OVA, the victim can track the suspect through the trial and afterward.

★ Witness Protection Program

If someone has information about a crime, the FBI may need to protect that person from harm. For that purpose, the FBI started the Witness Protection Program. This allows witnesses to escape to a new home and a new life.

FBI headquarters in Puerto Rico. This is just one of the more than fifty "Legal Attaches," or field offices of the FBI, stationed in United States embassies around the world.

Witnesses can use the program to stay hidden. They move far from people they have helped to bring to justice. They can live in a new state, or sometimes a new country, where they assume a new identity. They are encouraged to keep this identity for the rest of their lives to avoid danger.

The FBI needs informants to investigate cases. Without the Witness Protection Program, many of these informants would not cooperate. Many federal crimes could not be solved and criminals would remain at large.

TIME LINE

1908—The Bureau of Investigation (BOI) is created as part of the Department of Justice. The bureau investigates white-collar crimes such as fraud and embezzlement.

1924—J. Edgar Hoover is named as the new director of the Bureau of Investigation. Hoover will remain in this post until his death in 1972.

1932—The Bureau of Investigation begins operating the Scientific Crime Detection Laboratory. This office applies the latest scientific methods and investigative techniques to solve important crimes.

1935—The Bureau of Investigation is renamed the Federal Bureau of Investigation (FBI).

1942—The Office of Strategic Services (OSS) is formed to undertake spying missions in Asia and Europe. William "Wild Bill" Donovan is named its first director. The OSS will cease operations in the fall of 1945 after the end of World War II in the Pacific theater.

1947—Congress passes the National Security Act, which creates the Central Intelligence Agency. The agency will carry out espionage missions in foreign countries.

1949—Director J. Edgar Hoover of the FBI begins the bureau's "Ten Most Wanted" list of dangerous criminals. The list will be posted in public places and lead to the arrest of hundreds of important suspects.

1952—The National Security Agency (NSA) is founded. Its task is the interception, decoding, and analysis of electronic signals, including radio, telephone, and satellite transmissions.

1972—The FBI Academy begins training future agents at its campus in Quantico, Virginia.

1974—After the Watergate scandal, which brings the resignation of President Richard Nixon, the CIA comes under investigation by Congress. Many secret operations come to light and Congress bans some of the CIA's activities.

2001—*September 11:* Four passenger jets are hijacked by terrorists in the northeastern United States. Two of the planes are deliberately crashed into the towers of the World Trade Center, and a third crashes into the Pentagon. A fourth plane crashes into a field in rural Pennsylvania. The attacks lead to the creation of the Office of Homeland Security, the precursor to the Department of Homeland Security.

2002—The Office of Homeland Security starts the Homeland Security Advisory System, a color-coded alert scale that advises citizens and government agencies of the likelihood of another terrorist attack.

2002—Congress passes the USA Patriot Act, which sets down new methods of investigation and coordination among federal agencies working to prevent acts of terrorism.

2003—*January 24:* The Department of Homeland Security (DHS) begins operations. President George W. Bush names Tom Ridge, a former governor of Pennsylvania, as the first director of the DHS.

2005—*January 11:* Michael Chertoff replaces Tom Ridge as secretary of the Department of Homeland Security.

2009—*January 21:* Janet Napolitano replaces Michael Chertoff as secretary of Homeland. She is the third and current United States Secretary of Homeland Security, serving in the administration of President Barack Obama.

Glossary

appeal—To ask that an appellate court review the verdict or sentence in a court case.

Bureau of Investigation (BOI)—A federal agency set up in 1908 to investigate fraud, forgery, and other "white-collar" crimes. In 1935, the BOI was renamed the Federal Bureau of Investigation (FBI).

Communism—A political system in which people believe that each citizen in a society should have equal wealth.

Counterterrorism Center (CTC)—A CIA bureau that deals with efforts to combat terrorism around the world.

Department of Homeland Security (DHS)—An agency formed after the attacks of September 11, 2001, to help protect the country from further terrorist attack.

Director of Central Intelligence Agency (DCI)—The head of the CIA, who is responsible for directing the agency's operations.

Directorate of Science and Technology—A CIA department that handles espionage equipment and technology.

ECHELON—A network of listening devices that allows the United States and its allies to intercept and share messages and electronic signals from targeted areas.

embassy—The residence and offices of an ambassador and other government workers living in a foreign country.

embezzlement—To profit from the sale of an item or property when the seller is not the rightful owner of that item or property.

Enigma—A coding device used by the Nazis to send and receive coded messages during World War II. The Enigma mechanism was solved by mathematicians working in England during the war, allowing Allied leaders to follow German military plans and movements.

executive order—A rule put into effect by the president of the United States that has the same force as the law. It is up to federal officials to enforce executive orders.

Federal Emergency Management Agency (FEMA)—A federal agency that prepares for and responds to natural and man-made disasters. The agency coordinates relief and rescue efforts undertaken by local police, fire, and medical units.

forgery—Falsifying documents or a signature.

fraud—A way of tricking someone to get them to give up money.

General Intelligence Division (GID)—A part of the Department of Justice that collected information on suspected Communists and anarchists. The GID began after World War I and its first head was J. Edgar Hoover.

Homeland Security Advisory System—A colored scale of five risk levels that guides the federal government to assess the possibility of a terrorist attack and the appropriate precautions to take.

Legal Attaches—Also known as "legats," FBI agents operating in foreign countries.

Office of Victim Assistance (OVA)—A division of the FBI which assists victims of crime by informing them of the status of the investigation and providing shelter and other assistance if necessary.

Office of Strategic Services (OSS)—An intelligence agency formed during World War II, the forerunner of the Central Intelligence Agency.

reconnaissance aircraft—Planes used for spying. Oftentimes, these planes are fitted with high-powered cameras.

Special Agent in Charge (SAC)—The FBI agent who manages one of the bureau's fifty-five field offices, directs investigations, and handles agents and staff.

Strategic Information and Operations Center (SIOC)—A data center used by the FBI during a national emergency or crisis, and which coordinates rescue, pursuit of suspects, and investigative work.

telex—A wire service which used electric typewriters to send and receive messages.

Transportation Security Administration (TSA)—A federal agency that is responsible for protecting major transportation systems, including airports, highways, railroads, and ports.

UKUSA Group—A group of English-speaking allies, including the United States, the United Kingdom, Canada, Australia, and New Zealand, that share electronic intelligence and cooperate in intercepting electronic signals.

USA Patriot Act—A federal law passed in 2002 and meant to combat terrorism by allowing federal agencies to share information and investigate individuals suspected of plotting or carrying out attacks on the United States.

warrant—A document that has been authorized by a judge which allows law enforcement personnel to search a residence or place of business.

Witness Protection Program—An office of the FBI that allows important witnesses in certain cases to assume a new identity.

Chapter Notes

Chapter 1. The Department of Homeland Security

1. Bill Sammon, *Fighting Back: The War on Terrorism from Inside the Bush White House* (Washington, D.C.: Regnery Publishing Inc., 2002), pp. 83–135.

2. Richard A. Clarke, *Against All Enemies: Inside America's War on Terror* (New York: Free Press, 2004), pp. 248–249.

3. "Chronology of Changes to the Homeland Security Advisory System," *Department of Homeland Security,* n.d., <http://www.dhs.gov/xabout/history/editorial_0844.shtm> (December 20, 2006).

4. "U.S. Senate Roll Call Votes 109th Congress 1st Session," *The United States Senate,* February 15, 2005, <http://www.senate.gov/legislature/LIS/roll_call_lists/roll_call_vote_cfm.cfm?congress=109&session=1&vote=00010> (April 6, 2007).

Chapter 2. Tasks of Homeland Security

1. Emergency Management Institute, "Welcome to the Emergency Management Institute," *Federal Emergency Management Agency,* n.d., <http://www.training.fema.gov/EMIweb/> (December 22, 2006).

2. *U.S. Customs and Border Protection,* n.d., <http://www.cbp.gov/> (December 22, 2006).

3. *Transportation Security Administration,* n.d., <http://www.tsa.gov/> (December 22, 2006).

4. Jumana Farouky, "Airline Terror Plot Foiled," *Time.com,* August 10, 2006, <http://www.time.com/time/nation/article/0,8599,1224967,00.html> (December 21, 2006).

5. "Permitted and Prohibited Items," *Transportation Security Administration,* n.d., <http://www.tsa.gov/travelers/airtravel/prohibited/permitted-prohibited-items.shtm> (December 22, 2006).

Chapter 3. The OSS and the CIA

1. Anthony Cave Brown, *The Last Hero: Wild Bill Donovan* (New York: Times Books, 1982), pp. 236–237.

2. Ibid., p. 801.

3. Christopher Andrew, *For the President's Eyes Only: Secret Intelligence and the American Presidency from Washington to Bush* (New York: HarperCollins Publishers, 1995), p. 251.

4. Ibid., p. 202.

5. Stansfield Turner, *Secrecy and Democracy: The CIA in Transition* (Boston: Houghton Mifflin, 1985), p. 2.

6. *National Counterterrorism Center,* n.d., <http://www .nctc.gov/> (December 21, 2006).

7. Ibid.

8. Richard D. Fisher, *China's Missile Over the Taiwan Strait: A Political and Military Assessment,* In James Lilley and Chuck Downs, eds., *Crisis in the Taiwan Strait* (Washington, D.C.: National Defense University Press, 1997), pp. 167–216.

Chapter 4. Working for the CIA

1. John K. Cooley, *Unholy Wars: Afghanistan, America, and International Terrorism,* 3rd ed. (Sterling, Va.: Pluto Press, 2002), p. 71.

2. Lindsay Moran, *Blowing My Cover: My Life as a CIA Spy* (New York: The Penguin Group, 2005), p. 33.

3. Allan A. Swenson and Michael Benson, *The Complete Idiot's Guide to the CIA* (Indianapolis, Ind.: Alpha Books, 2003), p. 268.

4. *Directorate of Science and Technology,* n.d., <https:// www.cia.gov/cia/dst/home.html> (December 20, 2006).

5. Swenson, p. 27.

6. Stansfield Turner, *Secrecy and Democracy: The CIA in Transition* (Boston: Houghton Mifflin, 1985), p. 263.

Chapter 5. The National Security Agency

1. FAS Project on Government Secrecy, "NSA Celebrates its Fiftieth Anniversary," *Secrecy News,* November 4, 2002,

<http://www.fas.org/sgp/news/secrecy/2002/11/110402
.html> (April 6, 2007).

2. Andy Reinhardt, "Alan Turing: Thinking Up
Computers," *Business Week,* May 10, 2004, <http://www
.businessweek.com/magazine/content/04_19/b3882029_
mz072.htm> (October 1, 2007).

3. Henry C. Clausen and Bruce Lee, *Pearl Harbor: The
Final Judgment* (New York: Da Capo Press, 2001), p. 42.

4. Jeffrey Richelson, ed., "The National Security Agency
Declassified," *George Washington University,* January 13, 2000,
<http://www.gwu.edu/~nsarchiv/NSAEBB/NSAEBB23/
index.html> (December 22, 2006).

5. Philip H. Melanson, *Secrecy Wars: National Security,
Privacy, and the Public's Right to Know* (Washington, D.C.:
Brassey's, 2002), p. 61.

6. National Security Agency/Central Security Agency,
"United States Signals Intelligence Directive 18," *George
Washington University,* July 27, 1993, <http://www.gwu
.edu/~nsarchiv/NSAEBB/NSAEBB23/07-01.htm>
(December 21, 2006).

7. James Bamford, *Body of Secrets: Anatomy of the
Ultra-Secret National Security Agency From the Cold War
Through the Dawn of a New Century* (New York: Doubleday,
2001), p. 427.

Chapter 6. Intercepts and Analysis

1. "Career Fields—Foreign Language," National Security
Agency, n.d., <http://www.nsa.gov/careers/careers_1.cfm>
(December 22, 2006).

2. James Bamford, *Body of Secrets: Anatomy of the
Ultra-Secret National Security Agency From the Cold War
Through the Dawn of a New Century* (New York: Doubleday,
2001), p. 419.

3. Ibid., pp. 484–485.

4. "Careers," *National Security Agency,* n.d., <http://www.nsa.gov/careers/index.cfm> (Decem-ber 20, 2006).

Chapter 7. The History of the FBI

1. Richard Gid Powers, *Secrecy and Power: The Life of J. Edgar Hoover* (New York: The Free Press, 1987), pp. 188–193.

2. Athan G. Theoharis and John Stuart Cox, *The Boss: J. Edgar Hoover and the Great American Inquisition* (Philadelphia: Temple University Press, 1988), pp. 55–56.

3. Anthony Summers, *Official and Confidential: The Secret Life of J. Edgar Hoover* (Higham, Mass.: Wheeler Publishing, 1993), p. 29.

4. Neil J. Welch and David W. Marston, *Inside Hoover's FBI: The Top Field Chief Reports* (Garden City, N.Y.: Doubleday, 1984), p. 17.

5. Powers, p. 183.

6. Theoharis and Cox, p. 171.

7. "The FBI's Ten Most Wanted Fugitives," *Federal Bureau of Investigation,* n.d., <http://www.fbi.gov/wanted/topten/> (January 13, 2012).

8. Thomas, "H.R. 3162," *The Library of Congress,* 2001, <http://thomas.loc.gov/cgi-bin/bdquery/z?d107:H.R.3162:> (December 20, 2006).

Chapter 8. How the FBI Works

1. Athan G. Theoharis, ed., *The FBI: A Comprehensive Reference Guide* (Westport, Conn.: Greenwood Publishing Group, Inc., 1998), p. 254.

2. Ronald Kessler, *The FBI: Inside the World's Most Powerful Law Enforcement Agency* (New York: Pocket Books, 1993), p. 169.

3. Ibid., p. 159.

4. "Strategic Information and Operations Center (SIOC) Fact Sheet," *Federal Bureau of Investigation,* n.d., <http://www.fbi.gov/hq/siocfs.htm> (December 20, 2006).

5. "Victim Assistance," *Federal Bureau of Investigation,* n.d., <http://www.fbi.gov/hq/cid/victimassist/home.htm> (December 20, 2006).

Further Reading

Baker, David. *CIA and FBI*. Vero Beach, FL: Rourke Pub Group, 2005

Donovan, Sandra. *Protecting America: A Look at the People Who Keep Our Country Safe*. Minneapolis, Minnesota: Lerner Publishing Group, 2003.

Fridell, Ron. *Spy Technology*. Minneapolis, Minnesota: Lerner Publishing Group, 2006.

Gilbert, Adrian. *Secret Agents*. Buffalo, New York: Firefly Books, Ltd., 2009

Grayson, Robert. *The FBI and National Security*. Broomall, PA: Mason Crest, 2009

King, Bart. *The Big Book of Spy Stuff*. Layton, Utah: Gibbs-Smith, 2011

Internet Addresses

NSA.Gov
This is the official home page for the National Security Agency and Central Security
<http://www.nsa.gov/>

USA.Gov
This link offers information about the Department of Homeland Security
<http://www.dhs.gov/index.shtm>

FBI.Gov
This is the official home page for the Federal Bureau of Investigation
<http://www.fbi.gov/about-us/intelligence/intelligence>

Index